Being Naked Shining

BEING
NAKED
SHINING

*Secret Conversation with Rinpoche
and Others*

TORKEL LUNDBERG

2022
GOLDEN DRAGONFLY PRESS

FIRST PRINT EDITION, March 2022
FIRST EBOOK EDITION, March 2022

Copyright © 2022 by Torkel Lundberg.
Art and photos by Torkel Lundberg.
Typeset in Sabon LT Pro and Gill Sans Nova.
All rights reserved.
No part of this publication may be reproduced or transmitted in
any form or by any means, electronic or otherwise, without prior
written permission by the copyright owner.

ISBN–13: 978–1–7330099–9–7
Library of Congress Control Number: 2021952146

Printed on acid-free paper supplied by a Forest Stewardship
Council-certified provider.

First published in the United States of America by Golden
Dragonfly Press, 2022.

www.goldendragonflypress.com

The contents of this slim volume came into being exclusively through listening, learning, borrowing, and gleaning from different kinds of teachers. My appreciation and gratitude to this golden chain of teachers are beyond what any words can express. If anything, I am perhaps a messenger of these.

From early on in childhood, my father taught me to observe and move quietly in the natural world and it came to be my primary inspiration, along with a few of the innumerable poets, seers, and givers of visions.

While I was working with documentary film in northern Sweden, Samí elders revealed mythical songs of their ancestral lands and animals.

Close friends urged me to continue writing and drawing. They taught me that I perceive beauty and a sense of belonging in everything I see.

My distinguished guru is now Ziji Rinpoche in the Dzogchen Lineage. I would not have written most, if any, of these words without her teachings and our secret conversation.

Contents

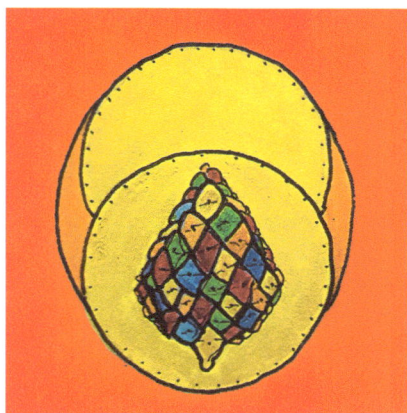

Heart bows for all ways beauty
the looking, crying of tears and smiling in me.
A sky of gratitude and love
in these tender whispers of secrets
irresistible as breathing
in this only place
I know and love.
The intimate in-shine, the natural course, the
outflow,
of wakeful lively knowing
and deepest care for all

My heart and my song
do not belong to me
Not even the veil of rings,
the garland of gems
or any wish-fulfilling tree

The softest lullaby ever known
the crucial intimacy of me and thee
golden beloved golden unity
brilliance bright

Awash in touch and soaring voice
old way of natural messaging
the whimper of cubs and fawns
a cosmic instinct and chalice of care

Following deer and bear
all sisters and brothers
Shining Naked Mother

Nature did this
devotion called me forth
naked, keening and clean
then spinning my being
a thread of ecstasy and dream

Is there anywhere
a thought boundless enough
for the essence
that fills me
awakened and alight?

I am the lightning
of thankfulness
I am the silence
where voices may sing

In the tender vessel
of my humming heart
there's nothing to fear.

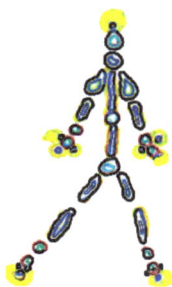

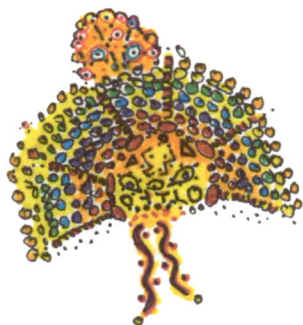

We are all invited
into this shining
open and wild.
The veils of self and other
slowly swinging
we are here
all seamlessly intermingling
and we are happy to stay
yes also, passing away.

We are all gathered
in the essence of clear meaning
the liveliness of light
blazing profusely throughout

Is there anywhere
a word magnificent enough
for this unbounded bliss
so rich and bright?

I dreamt of extinct creatures
small dinosaurs who delivered teachings
instructed me to serve truth and being
in all ways that I can.
They told me I am open to nature,
and need no teaching
for it is native in me

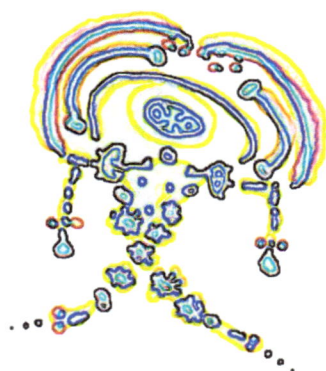

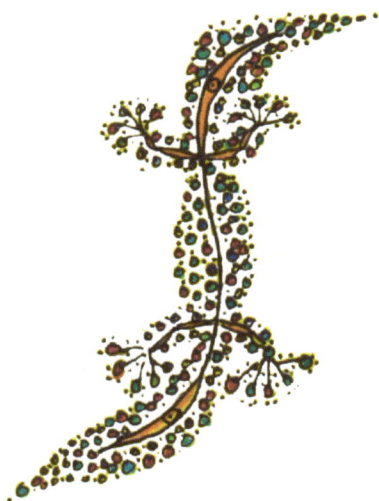

And in the dream humanoid extraterrestrials
taught me humility,
not to touch them,
nor to doubt their existence
never hurt or harm

The academicians of
Modern Scientific Method
predicting run-away mass extinction
within this century
or even less than one decade.

The lamas of
Old School Great Perfection
proclaiming pure perfect presence
oneness and concord
right now.

Lighting the wood-stove sauna
talking and singing by fire for
hours on end,
forgetting rich sparkling time

Then stepping out after midnight,
a solitary thrush softly calling
ringing an invisible path among stars
and the trees secretly shedding their foliage,
settling in near silence by our feet

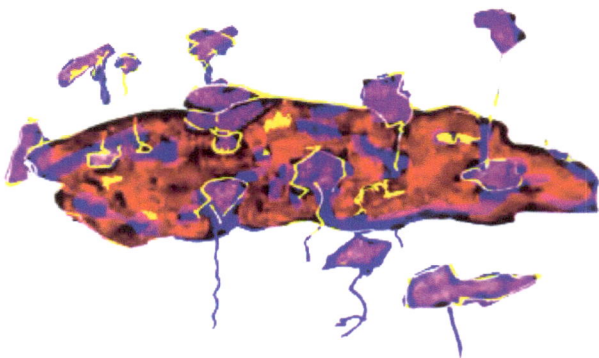

I saw a crow
dipping its beak into
a mirror of sky.
The empty clear crow
took a sip of water
then flew off
leaving no trace

All new, fresh
shifting clouds
and silent snow,
ice-sealed waters roaring.
The deep clear mountain streams
waking up as the echo
of the air I breathe

Idly longing
walking this earthen road,
geese greeting eyes and ears overhead
and passerines of every kind
flushing gold and jewelry
at my feet

Roused before dawn
in the depths of the dream
we had a chance meeting
and a few words were spoken, then silence

 fell again.

I thought of the old way of Sámi Joik
their bursts of spontaneous song.
The poets could place their ear to the ground and
listen to catch these magical sounds.
They say the joik originates at the heart of the world
at times in the heart-beat of a young reindeer
Now I know why the old poets and seers

 of Scandinavia

moved so deep into the untamed naked mountains
and prostrated with water stone and sky
in the grace of indivisibility
impermanence and permanence
join in blissful union
in the secret rapture of what is wild and will last.

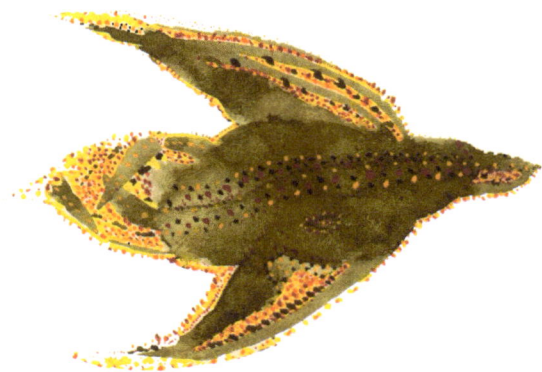

The wild bird,
in the clear black night
feasting on the moon's glitter,
calls to me again and again
establishing my place in the natural order,
then leaving no trace
the bird heads home

the wild bird,
soaking in the whisper of early bright
calling me over and over;
nothing whatsoever needs to be done
then, without a trace
the bird is gone

a tree of song

Migratory birds without hesitation
leaving their well-known summer lands
sun and stars giving a cue
trusting the inner compass
and their own soft calls, they fly

And sedentary, resident birds,
without the shadow of thought or worry, remain
in what is known so well, alive
undergoing inconceivable transformation,
a dome of darkness and silence
the gift of their natal home

Yet other birds, since time immemorial drifters
the vagrants glimpsed on a windy day, perhaps
in a tree laden with winter's fruit,
or in bushes heavy with the season's berries,
oh song of the prosperous land

This golden morning
everything born anew
from a spark so slight,
a whole new vista
born out of this
that is me and you

Within this empty lively picture
of primordial grace and joy,
through this luminous fabric of being
Ignis and *Phoenix* resound
indwelling purity source
the direct display of sacred intent
with the inherent option of choice

like the garuda
full-bodied
fully endowed
from beginning-less beginning
once upon a time
always
right now
the mighty bird
breaking the shell
hatching sun
egg-yellow
the strong wings
of impeccable flight
alight

My great fortune is to not have gone too crazy
for prestige, power, and money
instead the reindeer nibble
at the tasty ornament of Earth itself

In the senses of this intense sanity
I see the reindeer showered
by beams of the sun

And the reindeer flows on, golden
with that gait of ease and sway
most probably I won't see them again
but I don't mind
since when I saw them
it was as the essence
just like they saw me

Strong wind bending the trees
but the trees don't mind
bending and swaying at ease.
My wooden cottage is trembling
it doesn't mind,
bend and sway
like the trees
it yields

In the back yard,
at the edge of the forest
away from the wind
birds seek refuge.
I hear their whispers
all through the rough, wide-awake night.
Inhabitants at place
in their own way of natural rest.
I am happy to say I have a place to call home
and turn to you
Beloved,
each moment
as night turns to day.

What gift and grace,
for each with ears
eyes or any senses.
I am washed to
tears by beauty.

You called me forth and
flung me into life
with this song
of call-and-response.

*In great equalness
and evenness everything
shines. Each and every
wrong is also right, yes
Bright*

Might it be said
that awareness and love
are like the paper
which these letters
are written upon?
They are inseparable

like the mirror
and its reflection,
I may turn away,
but it's not gone.

Deer, leaping and gorgeous,
softly saluting something unheard.
An ancient language of muffled voices,
inwardly calling out, in elegance rejoicing.

The delicacy of their watchful bodies, the
flow of the flock
along interwoven pathways
with eyes vividly mild

This is where they simply roam,
an effortless journey, drifting across
endless golden edible floss.
In open vast sanctity,
where silence is actually heard
and water is drunk
straight from the stream

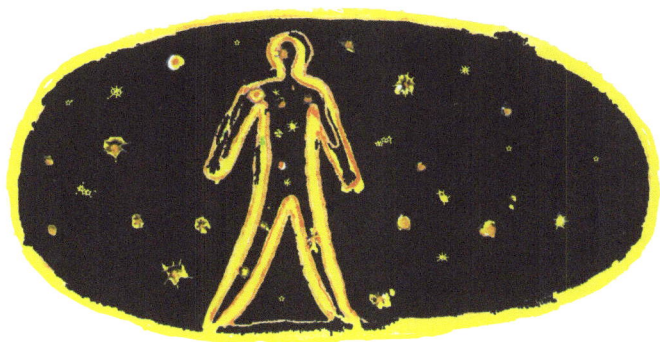

We smile in this presence
nourished and deeply relaxed, the
universe unfolding breathless
chanting, bowing and sensing
wherever we are.

We host the stars of sky within,
without any floor, walls or
ceiling.
We are a fool alone
with freedom in
each perception,
curious children
of what is
the very core.

It is our lamp
and we are its song,
to think otherwise
may be very lonely.

Oh this singular
humbling blessing
forever vast
glowing and strong
and mind, nature,
always with
many a hidden song

Uncontained is
all I hold dearly

Remember, you whispered, when going along:

the Bright exists, built entirely out of
compassionate humility
and alert awake knowing

soft, wet tongues of exceptional tide
touching on hidden aspects of vision
soaking sensory perceptions
in the qualities of opening heart

then falling back as they evolve
not too far, like the gentle swell of
the incoming tide of the ocean
slowly, steadily
lapping farther
up the beach

At one moment
I chose to be open
it was as if honesty
was all I had
the phases of constant youth
sweet animal tissue,
100% illumined
without any need
to explain

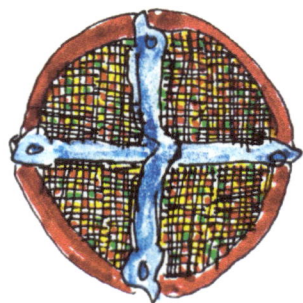

Why I go outdoors
or stay in
lucid pure space,
allowing
nature to enter
deep ventilation
opening
opening
through which they
may fly

someone called
redbreast robin
delivering showers of silver notes
shining in the resonant morning
a vulnerable messenger
freely giving of the forest's trees

flying out
within this open
the flycatcher
blue-tit
and raven
all of their kin
soar in song
giving over
in robes of
flawless sensitive feathers

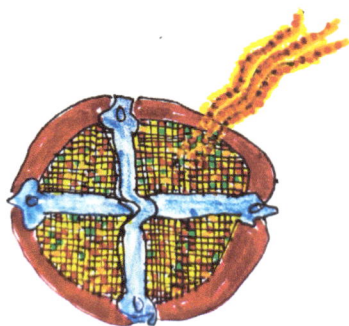

in spring
all of a sudden
as the thrushes start to sing
this is spring
yes the voice of the world
singing up

ahh this secret sacred voice
enshrined in living refuge
not secret nor sacred
not not sacred or secret
the perfect mandala
wholly pure strong
bursts of sound, sheer brilliance and all the power,
love, light and knowledge transmitted.

and the plants are shining
listen to them
blinking in the night

As I gently settle into the nature of things
I find myself more quiet and heeding
with markedly less to claim,
speaking up only on occasion.

Yes, my voice is calmer and more discreet,
perhaps like ripples on the surface of open water
or grasses imperceptibly quivering in the breeze,
with brief or no commentary
aroused to what actually is

The intimacy
in a world of breathtaking ease
with galaxies and universes pulling inward
and expanding outward,
always new songs
in this bubble of seeming life.
Dissolution, resolution,
falling inward, out of myself,
chanting a chorus of belonging
with beloved intoning friends

in the long shadow
whilst profoundly dreaming
I sink into a sweep of numinous
signaling and meaning,
now entering the luminous
night without a name

Dark dwelling
a shelter in a small forest clearing
in silken sonorous night. Afterwards you
told me
that you were ready
to leave your body
I took your hand.
Crystal snowflakes
slowly falling
in the Great Galaxy
which are we

Let's go naked,
as we came
lying down
sitting up
or moving

and in the dark boulder-sized pearls come
dancing slow motion
as if in oil
actually bouncing
into position
building a protective wall

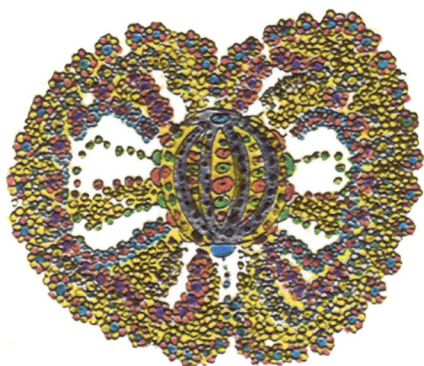

I see you sitting
legs folded
face smile of rapture
all pearly pure white
elevated and alive

We soar
lying down
or sitting

a shifting animal shape
quick silver quick
leaping out of the blue
swift leaps over me
feeling its whiskers
it dives into you

in that moment I told you
your hand on my shoulder is
spotted like a feral cat's

my hand holds you
as if I have the claws of an eagle
my fingers
are talons

We were forever
given brightness
and all worlds seem to know.
I am naturally drawn into wordlessness
and my eyes deepen in response.
I chose to live close to nature,
a lifestyle perfect for endless luminosity
as some of the oldest teachings and texts
suggest.

There is nothing to regret, nothing
to turn away from, nothing
to forgive or forget,
just keeping a diary of nature's
indescribable shine.

It is stunning to realize
that the most vigorous wild dove
high and elated, on the wing
in the deep azure above
and the sick, dull city pigeon
limping on the dirty pavement
as busy pedestrians hurry by
are of the same sublime essence,
all indivisible, like the blue and clear sky
and unceasingly exalted, just like us

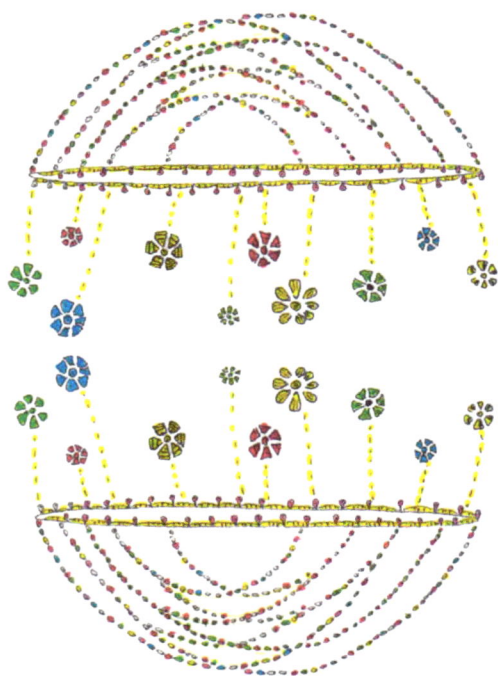

There is only blessing,
only blessings, gratitude and love remain.
Thank You
heart's deepest bows
for all ways expressing
the dazzling vibrancy
of emptiness alive,
holding in place
the secret, secure linkage
of the Sublime Lineage
in the Family and Friendship of
Being

The Well of Being

About the Author

TORKEL LUNDBERG is a freelance nature documentary film maker. He also conducts field work monitoring seals and porpoises in the waters around Sweden. This is his first published collection of images and text. He currently lives in a small cottage in central Sweden.

Acknowledgements

Thanks to Gunilla Hamne, Fredrik Pleijel, Peter Amoghli, Björn Ola Lind, for encouragement and inspiration.

Alice Maldonado, my publisher at Golden Dragonfly Press, for bearing with me through thick and thin in the design and completion of this book.

Vajra friends, sisters and brothers, for connection and song.

www.ingramcontent.com/pod-product-compliance
Lightning Source LLC
Chambersburg PA
CBHW042124080426
42733CB00002B/6